W9-DIL-450

DISCARD

A TRUE BOOK™

The Georgia Colony

KEVIN CUNNINGHAM

Children's Press®
An Imprint of Scholastic Inc.
New York   Toronto   London   Auckland
Mexico City   New Delhi   Hong Kong
Danbury, Connecticut

Content Consultant
Jeffrey D. Kaja, PhD
Assistant Professor of History
California State University, Northridge

Library of Congress Cataloging-in-Publication Data

Cunningham, Kevin, 1966–
   The Georgia colony/Kevin Cunningham.
      p. cm.—(A true book)
   Includes bibliographical references and index.
   ISBN-13: 978-0-531-25389-2 (lib. bdg.)   ISBN-13: 978-0-531-26602-1 (pbk.)
   ISBN-10: 0-531-25389-2 (lib. bdg.)   ISBN-10: 0-531-26602-8 (pbk.)
   1. Georgia—History—Colonial period, ca. 1600–1775—Juvenile literature. I. Title. II. Series.
   F289.C86 2011
   975.8'02—dc22   2011008351

975.8
cun
4/14
$15.00
Follett

Find the Truth!

Everything you are about to read is true *except* for one of the sentences on this page.

Which one is **TRUE**?

T or F   James Oglethorpe's colony had a strong government.

T or F   Slavery played a large part in Georgia farming after 1750.

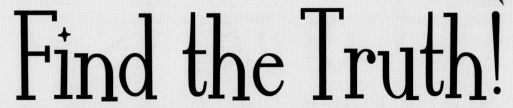

Find the answers in this book.

3

Contents

1 Georgia Before the Europeans

How did Hernando de Soto's arrival damage
Native American communities?. 7

2 Troubled Colony

What help did Georgia settlers get from others?. . . . 15

3 Life in Colonial Georgia

What kind of jobs did colonists
do in early Georgia?. 21

4 Royal Colony

What changed in Georgia
after James Oglethorpe
left? 27

**5 The American
Revolution**

Did all Georgians agree to
fight against Britain? 33

The Declaration of Independence

THE **BIG** TRUTH!

Georgia's Founding Fathers

What did Georgia's founders do after
the American Revolution?........................**38**

True Statistics........... **43**

Resources **44**

Important Words........ **46**

Index **47**

About the Author........ **48**

Colonial blacksmiths were often also the town dentist.

Timeline of Georgia Colony History

9,000 B.C.E.

Native Americans begin living in the Georgia area.

1539

Spanish explorer Hernando de Soto enters Georgia.

1733

Englishman James Oglethorpe founds the Georgia Colony.

1751

Slavery is legalized in Georgia.

1788

Georgia approves the U.S. Constitution.

CHAPTER 1

Georgia Before the Europeans

Thousands of years before Europeans arrived and began to colonize Georgia, Native Americans had moved into the area. By the time Spanish explorers arrived in the mid-1500s, several local native groups had joined into a **confederacy** called the Muskogee, or Creek. They settled in small *italwa*, or villages, and lived in houses of wood and mud. They grew crops such as rice and maize (corn). Each village had an open area for meetings, games, and ceremonies called a *pascova*.

The people in a Creek village chose a *mico*, or chief. His job was to deal with outsiders in matters such as trade and warfare. The mico did not force villagers to follow his decisions. Instead, he persuaded them. Even then, leaders of family clans, usually older women, limited the mico's authority. Though the Creek fought wars, sometimes they settled their disagreements with foes in a game of *toli*, a lacrosse-like sport.

The Creek chose strong, smart men to serve as micos.

The Cherokee

One of the Creek's most powerful neighbors was the Tsalagi, or Cherokee. The Cherokee pushed into the Creek homeland after being forced out of areas farther north. Cherokee farmers grew maize, beans, and squash. These are called the Three Sisters. In Cherokee culture, women farmed the fields and gathered berries and wild plants. Men hunted deer and other game, and when necessary, went to war.

The name Cherokee comes from the Creek language and means "people of different speech."

Georgia's fertile soil provided the Cherokee with bountiful crops of maize.

Cherokee villages, surrounded by tall fences, were easily defended against enemies.

The Cherokee built a large council house in the center of their villages for meetings and religious ceremonies. Thirty to 60 dome-shaped houses were erected around the council house. They were built of clay and sticks plastered onto a wooden frame.

The Cherokee eventually pushed the Creek farther south. Before that, another people appeared on the scene. Their arrival would be disastrous for the Creek and Cherokee.

The Europeans Arrive

In the years after Christopher Columbus came to the Americas in 1492, Europeans slowly explored North America. They generally had little interest in the land that is now Georgia. Instead, they kidnapped Indians in the area, such as the Yamasee, to work as slaves in Spanish **colonies** in the Caribbean. In 1539, Spanish explorer Hernando de Soto arrived in the region with 600 soldiers in search of silver and gold.

Before coming to North America, de Soto helped conquer the Inca people in South America.

Hernando de Soto first landed on the coast of present-day Florida.

De Soto traveled through the present-day southern and southeastern regions of the United States. At times, he had peaceful relations with native peoples. Often, however, his army robbed, enslaved, and killed Native Americans. But the Spaniards' most destructive action was accidental. De Soto's army had carried European diseases that the Indians could not fight off. In some places, 90 percent of the Indian population may have died from these diseases.

Many Indians died of smallpox, which covers the body in a painful rash.

Diseases such as measles and whooping cough proved fatal to the Indians.

The British and the Indians had useful items to trade with one another.

The British Arrive

In 1674, English traders entered the area eager to trade with the Creek and Cherokee. The British exchanged cloth and metal goods with Indians for deerskins. They also traded for slaves that the Indians had taken from enemy peoples. At the time, the English were settled in South Carolina, and the Spanish were in Florida. Each began to see the Georgia region as a place of future settlement.

NORTH CAROLINA

Appalachian Mountains

CHEROKEE

Rome

UPPER CREEK

Original
13 Colonies

Area
enlarged

SOUTH
CAROLINA

Heard's Fort □

Augusta

Oconee River

Ogeechee River

Savannah River

Macon

Ocmulgee River

LOWER CREEK

GEORGIA

Savannah · ■ ⟶ Fort Moore

Tybee Island

Altamaha River

Darien ·

■ Fort Frederica

Colonial boundaries

Present boundaries

Satilla River

St. Marys River ⟶ Cumberland Island

0 ___ miles ___ 50
0 ___ km ___ 50

SPANISH TERRITORY

ATLANT
OCEAN

CHAPTER 2

Troubled Colony

In January 1733, an Englishman named James Oglethorpe led 114 British settlers up the Savannah River. He established a colony and named it Georgia, after Great Britain's King George II. Oglethorpe hoped to create a place for Britain's poor to get a fresh start. He belonged to a council of **trustees** that made the colony's rules. But all the other council members lived in Britain, so Oglethorpe served as Georgia's day-to-day leader.

The colony's motto was "Not for ourselves, but for others."

Mary Musgrove

Mary Musgrove was a trader who settled on the Savannah River with her husband in about 1717. Her father was British and her mother was Yamacraw Creek. The Indians knew her as Coosaponakeesa. When Oglethorpe arrived, Musgrove helped him communicate with the local Native Americans by acting as his translator. She also set up a trading post that brought Indian and British traders together. She remained a well-known Georgian figure until her death in the 1760s.

The Georgian trustees gave each male colonist 50 acres (20 hectares) of land at the end of the first year of settlement. Five acres (2 ha) were located in Savannah, the colony's main town. Forty-five acres (18 ha) were in the country, where crops and farm animals could be raised. Oglethorpe worked to build good relationships with Native Americans. Chief Tomochichi's Yamacraw Creek people even taught the settlers how to grow native crops.

Tomochichi and his son Toonahowi were both close lifetime allies of Oglethorpe.

Georgian colonists had a friendly relationship with the native peoples.

Many new settlers arrived in the early years of the colony.

Parliament, Britain's **legislature**, sent money every year to help the colony. No other British colony received such a payment. But even with the funds, and despite Oglethorpe's good intentions, Georgia suffered serious problems. Crops failed because many settlers either did not know how to farm or refused to work the fields. Disease was a constant threat, and fresh water was hard to find. Spain threatened to invade the region to set up its own colonies.

Unhappiness

Georgia did not have a local government to solve problems, set up schools, or build roads. Trustees were making decisions far away in England. The lack of leadership created tension. Many settlers disliked the trustees' rules, especially the ban on liquor and slaves. In the 1730s, people began to leave the colony. The trustees, fearing the colony would fail, replaced Oglethorpe in 1743.

Today, Savannah is home to more than 130,000 people.

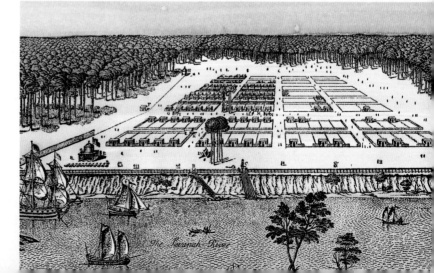

Savannah was the first planned city in America.

Savannah's port first opened in 1744.

CHAPTER 3

Life in Colonial Georgia

There were, however, signs of hope in Georgia. Augusta had grown into a successful trading town. Savannah had a courthouse and a jail, and there was a public flower garden that settlers could enjoy. Trading ships stopped regularly in Savannah after local **merchants** set up for business in 1744. Georgians sold products such as dried meat and lumber to other colonies and to Britain. In return, merchants brought in coffee, sugar, clothing, and furniture.

 Savannah remains a major port city today.

Colonial women used spinning wheels to make yarn.

Women in the Colony

Women in the colony cared for the children, cleaned the home, cooked, and made clothes. On farms, they plowed, planted, and picked crops. Only a few women, such as Mary Musgrove, became traders or operated a business. Women could not own land. If a landowner without sons died, the land went back to the trustees. The colonists eventually pressured the trustees into changing this rule.

Farmers, Traders, Frontiersmen

In the colony's early days, most men tried to farm. A few traded with the Indians. As Savannah grew, it attracted men who worked at specialized trades such as barrel making, shoemaking, and tailoring. These tradesmen taught their skills to boys, who started their own businesses after years of training. A small number of settlers moved to the undeveloped rural areas beyond Augusta to carve out farms on the **frontier**.

Most metal items were made from iron during colonial times.

Blacksmiths created metal products such as horseshoes and tools.

Children from nearby farms traveled to local schools.

A Georgian Childhood

Boys chopped firewood and helped their fathers on the farm. Girls learned cooking, cleaning, and sewing from their mothers. Because Georgia's trustees did not provide schools, settlers at first taught their children at home. In time, schools known as old-field schools were established. These one-room buildings were erected in unused fields. Teachers presented simple lessons to the students, because most schools had few books and no paper, pencils, or other supplies.

Slavery

Because of pressure from settlers, Georgia's trustees lifted the ban on slaves in 1751. By 1775, about 18,000 slaves were living in Georgia. Colonial law considered slaves property. Owners could sell slaves and take them away from their families. Slaves were often treated very harshly. They ate poorly, had little to wear, and lived in simple shacks or cabins. Children of slaves were also considered slaves.

Some slaves worked in the field while others worked in colonists' houses.

After the settlement of Savannah, slaves were used to clear land and tend cattle.

Georgians elected wealthy landowners to important political positions.

CHAPTER 4

Royal Colony

In June 1752, the British government took over responsibility for Georgia from the trustees. Settlers asked Parliament to declare Georgia a royal colony separate from neighboring South Carolina. In 1754, Parliament granted their request. The same year, a general assembly was established in Georgia. This local government had two levels, or houses. Britain's Royal Crown approved the officials in the upper house. The lower house was made up of representatives elected by Georgians.

Most of Georgia's political leaders were slave owners.

Voting and Expansion

Male landowners were the only colonists allowed to vote. Those who owned more than 500 acres (202 ha) of land could run for office. As the colony grew, Georgia's borders expanded to Saint Marys River to the south and the Mississippi River to the west. The **economy** also changed. Large farms called plantations were established. They grew valuable crops such as rice and indigo, a plant used to make blue dye.

Plantations often had large houses where the owners and their families lived.

Slaves were not allowed to learn to read or write.

Slave labor contributed to the success of the Georgian economy.

Slavery Grows

Georgia's slaves first arrived from other colonies and islands in the Caribbean. But huge plantations required more slaves. Beginning in 1766, slave ships full of Africans began docking in Savannah. The Africans who survived the harsh, cruel journey were sold at slave auctions. By 1800, Georgia's slave population was almost 30,000. The plantation owners put most of these slaves to work farming the rice and indigo.

Stamps were a common method of taxation in Great Britain.

Colonists set fires to protest the Stamp Act.

Patriots and Loyalists

In the 1760s, the British needed money to pay their war debts. Parliament turned to their American colonies. In 1764, English lawmakers placed taxes on the sugar, molasses, and rum that were brought into Georgia. The Stamp Act of 1765 required all colonists to buy a special stamp to be placed on printed materials. These included legal documents, magazines, and newspapers. Colonists were angered because they had no voice in the legislature making the rules. The colonists called it "taxation without representation."

Displeased colonists burn stamps in protest.

Though displeased about the taxes, Georgia remained loyal to Britain. Frontier settlers relied on British soldiers for protection. The colony's economy depended on selling products to British customers. But the taxes started affecting merchants and rich plantation farmers. Many Georgians began to side with the Patriots. These were colonists who opposed British rule. Georgians began to split between the Patriots and the Loyalists, or those who wanted to remain under Britain's rule.

The Continental Congress was attended by important leaders such as George Washington and John Adams.

There were 56 representatives at the First Continental Congress.

The American Revolution

Parliament withdrew the Stamp Act four months after passing it but continued to impose other taxes, including a tax on tea. In September 1774, representatives from 12 colonies attended the First Continental Congress in Philadelphia to discuss a course of action. Georgia, busy defending its frontier against Native American attack, was the only colony that did not attend the meeting. Georgian leaders, however, held their own First Provincial Congress in January 1775. The majority of those who attended voted to remain loyal to Britain.

Colonial militiamen defeated British troops at Concord.

On April 19, 1775, British troops clashed with colonial militia at Lexington and Concord in Massachusetts. Battles in Boston soon followed. People throughout the 13 colonies prepared for war with the British. Even in Georgia, the Patriot cause was gaining support. On July 4, 1775, Georgia held its Second Provincial Congress. After two weeks of meetings, the Congress created a state government. It also elected three representatives to the Continental Congress.

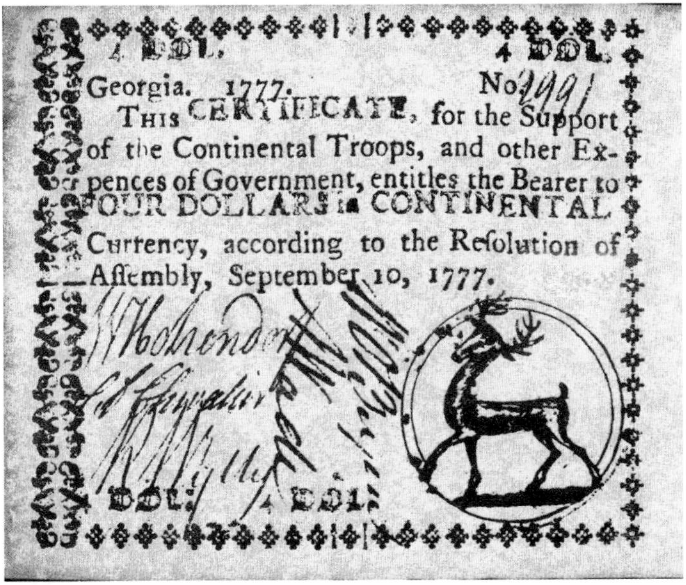
4 DOL.
4 DOL.
Georgia. 1777. No 2991
THIS CERTIFICATE, for the Support of the Continental Troops, and other Ex-pences of Government, entitles the Bearer to FOUR DOLLARS in CONTINENTAL Currency, according to the Refolution of Affembly, September 10, 1777.
DOL.
4 DOL.

During the 1770s, Georgia printed its own banknotes to help pay for the war.

Split in Two

Georgians remained divided on the issue of seeking **independence** from Britain. Neighbors took opposing sides. Families, friendships, and businesses broke up. Some colonies resented Georgia's hesitation to join the fight against the British. South Carolina threatened to stop trade with Georgia. But ill feelings faded when Georgia's three representatives approved the Declaration of Independence.

Victories on Both Sides

By early February 1776, a fleet of British warships had landed on Tybee Island, Georgia. Their goal was to buy rice and other supplies in Savannah and carry them back to British forces in Boston. But on March 3, 1776, 600 Patriot militiamen attacked the vessels and set three of them on fire. The victory ended British control of Savannah until December 1778, when the British easily recaptured the city.

A member of the 1st Georgia Continental infantry loads his gun.

Elijah Clarke

Elijah Clarke rose from being a poor Georgia frontiersman to becoming a hero of the American Revolutionary War. In 1780, Clarke led a **militia** charge against the British at Kettle Creek, Georgia. He spent the next several months raiding British and Loyalist troops in the Carolinas. At Musgrove Hill, South Carolina, he commanded a successful cavalry attack against British forces. In 1781, Clarke led one of the armies that recaptured Augusta from the British.

Georgia's Founding Fathers

Peter Tondee was the owner of the tavern where the Second Provincial Congress met in 1775 to establish a state government in Georgia. Tondee was a master carpenter dedicated to the American cause of independence. From 1774 to 1775, he hosted debates on Georgia's role in the colonies' dealings with Britain. Debaters discussed whether Georgia should participate in the First Continental Congress and if Georgians should join the Sons of Liberty. This was a group of Patriots that formed to protect the rights of colonists.

Button Gwinnett

Button Gwinnett was the second man to sign the Declaration of Independence, after John Hancock. Born in Britain, Gwinnett was a successful American plantation owner. He was Georgia's second governor and wrote an early version of Georgia's state constitution.

Lyman Hall

Lyman Hall was a physician and clergyman. Hall attended the Second Continental Congress and was a signer of the Declaration of Independence. He later served as Georgia's governor and helped create the University of Georgia.

George Walton

George Walton was a lawyer in Savannah. At 26 years of age, he was one of the youngest signers of the Declaration of Independence. When Britain recaptured Savannah in December 1778, he was taken prisoner for 10 months. Later, he was Georgia's governor, a U.S. senator, and chief justice of the Georgia Supreme Court.

Georgia's War

After regaining Savannah, British forces captured many towns, including Augusta. In 1779, American forces, along with French soldiers aiding the colonists' fight, attempted to retake Savannah. The failed monthlong battle was one of the bloodiest of the war. American and French losses included about 1,000 dead, wounded, or taken prisoner. By 1781, however, the Americans had begun to overpower the British in battle after battle. The Americans were getting closer to winning the war.

General Pulaski eventually died of wounds he suffered fighting for Savannah.

Georgia citizens were forced to fight off British troops after the war ended.

Victory

On October 19, 1781, the British surrendered to the Americans at Yorktown, Virginia. Nine months later, American forces pushed out British troops still holed up in Savannah. But the war had left many parts of the colonies in ruins. Many Georgian homes were burned, crops were damaged, and plantations were destroyed. Thousands of slaves and Loyalists left Georgia. Many went to Britain. Georgia was in worse shape than ever.

William Few's brother had been hanged before the war for protesting against British taxes.

William Few went on to serve as a U.S. senator, a Georgia state representative, and a judge.

Next Steps

Georgia slowly attracted new colonists and tradesmen to help repair the war's damage. Georgians relied heavily on slave labor to rebuild its plantation system. In 1787, the former colonies sent representatives to Philadelphia to write a constitution for the new United States. Georgians William Few and Abraham Baldwin signed the document before it was sent to each state for approval. On January 2, 1788, Georgian officials approved the U.S. Constitution, and Georgia became the fourth U.S. state. ★

Number of houses in a Cherokee village: 30 to 60

Number of soldiers in Hernando de Soto's army: 600

Number of settlers with James Oglethorpe: 114

Number of acres given to a male colonist after one year: 50 acres (20.2 ha)

Year Georgia became a royal colony: 1754

Number of months Britain kept the Stamp Act: 4

Number of Georgians who signed the Declaration of Independence: 3

Number of militiamen who burned British rice boats: 600

Number of states that approved the Constitution before Georgia: 3

Did you find the truth?

F James Oglethorpe's colony had a strong government.

T Slavery played a large part in Georgia farming after 1750.

Resources

Books

Harkins, Susan S., and William H. Harkins. *Georgia: The Debtors Colony*. Hockessin, DE: Mitchell Lane, 2006.

Lommel, Cookie. *James Oglethorpe: Humanitarian and Soldier*. Philadelphia: Chelsea House, 2000.

Pancella, Peggy. *Hernando de Soto*. Mankato, MN: Heinemann Library, 2003.

Santella, Andrew. *The Cherokee*. New York: Children's Press, 2000.

Schumacher, Tyler. *The Georgia Colony*. Mankato, MN: Capstone, 2006.

Sonneborn, Liz. *The Creek*. New York: Lerner, 2006.

Stechschulte, Pattie. *Georgia*. New York: Children's Press, 2008.

Todd, Anne M. *The Cherokee: An Independent Nation*. Mankato, MN: Capstone, 2000.

Organizations and Web Sites

Cherokee Nation

www.cherokee.org

Learn about Cherokee history and culture, and find out what's going on today on the Cherokee Reservation in Tahlequah, Oklahoma.

Georgia Historical Society

www.georgiahistory.com

Search the society's Web site for historical maps and other helpful information to learn about Georgia's history.

Places to Visit

Augusta Museum of History

560 Reynolds Street
Augusta, GA 30901
(706) 722-8454
www.augustamuseum.org
Study exhibits that tell the story of Augusta from prehistory through colonial times and into the present.

Savannah History Museum

303 Martin Luther King, Jr. Boulevard
Savannah, GA 31401
(912) 651-6825
www.chsgeorgia.org
/home.cfm/page
/SavannahHistoryMuseum.htm
Explore the history of Savannah since its founding through artifacts and hands-on exhibits.

Important Words

colonies (KAH-luh-neez) — areas settled by people from another country and controlled by that country

confederacy (kuhn-FED-ur-uh-see) — a number of groups or countries that gather together to help one another

constitution (kahn-sti-TOO-shuhn) — the laws of a country that state the rights of the people and the powers of government

economy (ih-KA-ne-mee) — the system of buying, selling, and making things and managing money

frontier (fruhn-TEER) — the far edge of a settled territory or country

governor (GUHV-uh-nhur) — a person who controls or exercises authority over an area

independence (in-di-PEN-duhns) — a state of not being controlled by others

legislature (LEJ-is-lay-chur) — a group of people who have the power to make or change laws

merchants (MUR-chuhntz) — people who buy and sell goods to make money

militia (muh-LISH-uh) — a group of people who are trained to fight but who aren't professional soldiers

trustees (truss-TEEZ) — people who watch the property and affairs of another company or other people

Index

Page numbers in **bold** indicate illustrations

agriculture, **9**, 17, 18, 22, 23, 24, **25**, **28**, 29, 31, 41
Augusta, Georgia, 21, 23, 34, 40

Baldwin, Abraham, 42
banknotes, **36**

Cherokee people, **9–10**, 13
children, 22, 23, **24**, 25
Clarke, Elijah, **37**
Columbus, Christopher, 11
Continental Congress, **32**, 33, 34, 38, 39
Creek people, 7–**8**, 9, 10, 13, 16, **17**

debates, **38**
Declaration of Independence, 35, 39
diseases, **12**, 18

economy, 28, **29**, 31
education, 19, **24**
elections, **26**, 27, 28, 34
European exploration, **6**, **11**–12

Few, William, **42**
foods, 7, **9**, 17

George II, king of England, 15
governors, 39
Great Britain, **13**, 15, 16, 18, 19, 21, 27, 29–30, 31, 34, 35, 36, 37, 38, 39, 40, **41**

Hall, Lyman, 39
houses, 7, **10**, **22**, 24, 25, 28, 41
hunting, 9

landowners, 22, **26**, 28
Loyalists, 31, 33, 37, 41

map, **14**
merchants, 21, 31

micos (chiefs), **8**
militias, **34**, 35, 37
Musgrove, Mary, **16**, 22

Oglethorpe, James, **6**, 15, 16, 17, 18, 19

Parliament, 18, 27, 30, 33
Patriots, 31, 37, 38
plantations, **28**, 29, 31, 39, 41, 42
Provincial Congress, 33, 35, 38
Pulaski, Casimir, **40**

Revolutionary War, **34**, 35, **36**, **40**, **41**

Savannah, Georgia, 17, **19**, **20**, 21, 23, **25**, 29, 34, 36, 39, 40, 41
Savannah River, 15, 16
slavery, **6**, 11, 12, 13, 19, **25**, 27, **29**, 41, 42
Sons of Liberty, 38
Soto, Hernando de, **6**, **11**–12
Stamp Act (1765), **30**, 33
statehood, 42

taxes, **30**–31, 33
Three Sisters, 9
timeline, **6**
Tomochichi (Creek chief), 17
Tondee, Peter, 34, 38
trade, 8, **13**, 16, 21, 22, 36
trades, **23**, 42
trustees, 15, 17, 19, 22, 24, 25, 27
Tybee Island, Georgia, 36

U.S. Constitution, **6**, 42

villages, 7–8, **10**

Walton, George, 39
Washington, George, **32**
women, 8, 9, **22**, 24

About the Author

Kevin Cunningham has written more than 40 books on disasters, the history of disease, Native Americans, and other topics. Cunningham lives near Chicago with his wife and young daughter.